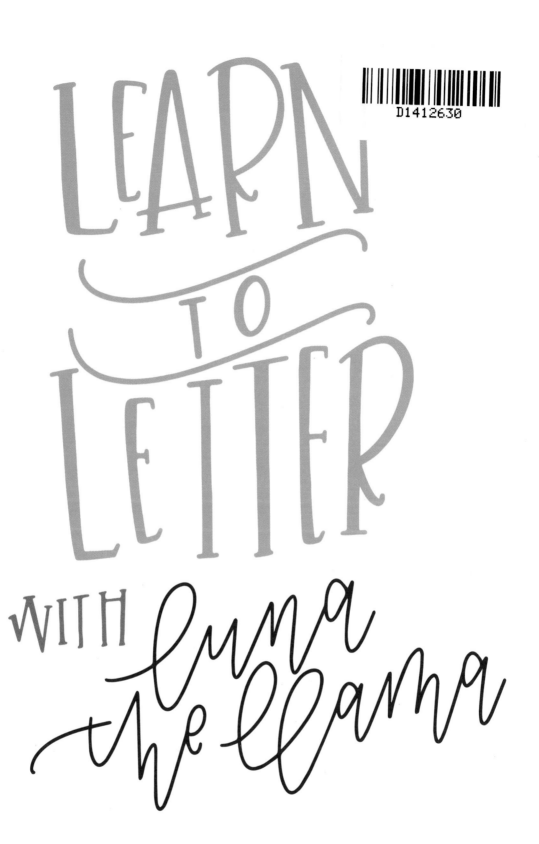

LEARN TO LETTER WITH Luna the Llama

A HAND-LETTERING WORKBOOK BY
BESTSELLING AUTHOR CHALKFULLOFLOVE

Paige Tate & Co. is an imprint of Blue Star Press

PO Box 8835, Bend, OR 97708

www.paigetate.com

For details or ordering information, email the publisher at

contact@paigetate.com.

Written by Chalkfulloflove

Illustrated by Chalkfulloflove and Kelsey Davis

ISBN: 9781944515904

Printed in Mexico

FOR MY DAUGHTER

emerson
coe

THIS BOOK

belongs to

HELLO

I'm
Sarah!

I'm
Luna!

Hey, you! So glad you picked up this book. Was it Luna the llama that drew you in? Luna is pretty cute and has that effect on you. She is going to take us through this book as we learn to letter! Who's excited?!

Can you believe that most schools don't teach cursive anymore? Maybe they think it was irrelevant or not important. I made a whole career out of it, so I think it's pretty important! You definitely don't have to make a career out of lettering, but you sure can do some fun things with it. Think of all those school projects you could make even better-looking or maybe you want to make a card for a friend, or even step up your sidewalk chalk game—the possibilities are endless. Why do you want to learn to letter?

I wanted to take a second to introduce myself. I am Sarah-aka-Chalkfullo-flove. For as long as I can remember I have always loved drawing, sketching, and lettering. I grew up waiting for the next poster board project in elementary school so I had a chance to decorate it.

I went to school for graphic communications, where I got to design and print so many fun projects. It was a dream come true. After graduating college, I spent a few years working graphic design jobs that were not the most fulfilling. I moved to a new city and found myself looking for a new creative outlet, and I discovered chalk lettering and modern calligraphy. On a whim in late 2013, I started a modest Etsy shop where I sold custom calligraphed wedding signs. That modest Etsy shop has grown into something I never thought could happen!

Enough about me. Let's introduce you to Luna! Luna is my lady llama friend who will be here every step of the way while we walk through the art of hand lettering! She is looking to up her craft game by learning some lettering. She wants to be able to make really cute cards for all of her friends. Don't worry, you'll meet them later!

Lettering might not come naturally to you, but don't get discouraged! It takes time to learn a new skill, and your pal Luna will be learning right along with you every step of the way.

Just remember these tips:

- Don't give up

- Practice makes progress

- Try your hardest

- All lettering is beautiful

TABLE OF CONTENTS

THE PLAN

I understand-you want to get to the good stuff. But before we can get there we gotta learn a few basics. We'll start by talking a little bit about where hand lettering came from, and then we'll go over a little lettering vocab, explore the best tools to use and the how-to of lettering, and do a little warm-up before getting into our letter drills! The letter drills make up the bulk of this book and will help you memorize the muscle movements needed to create beautiful letters over and over! We'll also chat about how to mix and match different styles, and then we'll put it all to the test with our activities. (That's when you get to meet Luna's friends!)

what is hand lettering?

Since I can remember, I have always enjoyed hand lettering. You might be wondering what the difference is between "hand lettering" and "handwriting." I like to think of lettering as drawing letters, versus writing them. Lettering puts an artistic spin on the letters we know and love! You can create really beautiful and fun pieces using the lettering techniques you'll be learning in this book. Lettering does take more time, skill, and patience than just writing something. We are going to go over how to master those skills and be patient with ourselves when learning, just like Luna!

HAND lettering   hand writing

Lettering styles came from written documents you might find in your history book. Ever heard of calligraphy? There are multiple types of calligraphy that have been used for centuries! We didn't always have computers to record our words. That job was done by scribes. Scribes were people who copied out documents, especially before printing was invented. As you can imagine, scribes probably had pretty good lettering skills. So, for years and years lettering has been passed down and reworked, and everyone can put their unique spin on it!

LETTER BASICS

SERIF H

Sometimes letters like to wear little shoes on their feet. We call those "serifs." Luna likes to include them on some of her letters to add a little decoration to them!

SANS SERIF G

Sans is French for "without." Therefore, a sans serif font has no feet! It is a personal favorite of mine to match with script lettering.

BASELINE m

The baseline is where the bottom of your letter sits.

MEANLINE

The meanline is half the distance from the base-line to the cap height.

DOWNSTROKE a

The downward stroke of the letter, which is the thickest part.

HAIRLINE l

Any upstrokes of calligraphy letters can be referred to as hairline strokes. This is the thinnest part of your letter.

CROSS STROKE t

The line that crosses through your letters. Think capital letters "A," "H," "F," and the lowercase letter "t." These can be as basic or as decorative as you like!

ASCENDER h

Extends above the meanline, and can be found in the letters "t," "h," "k," and "l."

DESCENDER g

Extends below the baseline and can be found in "g," "y," "p," "q," and "j."

13

LETTERING TOOLS

What I love about this style of lettering is the ability to use whatever tool I want! In the next few pages, I am sharing my favorite pens and markers that I use to letter and draw. Feel free to try out any others that catch your eye!

letter

Tombow TwinTone Markers: What makes these pens so cool is they have two different sizes—thick and thin! They are a fiber-based tip and use water-based ink. Perfect for writing in your notebook!

Crayola Super Tips: With a little pressure, these markers can go from a thick to thin line–no problem! And even better, they are washable. So Luna doesn't have to worry if she gets it on her fur!

letter

Crayola Broad Line markers: You are probably pretty familiar with this classic marker! They are perfect for drawing and lettering on a larger scale, like school projects and poster boards!

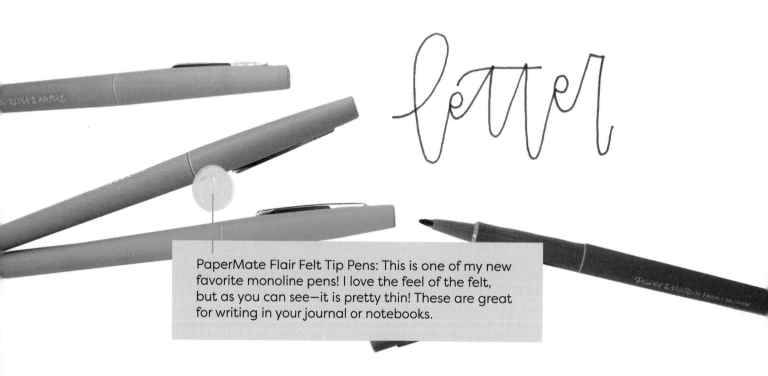

PaperMate Flair Felt Tip Pens: This is one of my new favorite monoline pens! I love the feel of the felt, but as you can see—it is pretty thin! These are great for writing in your journal or notebooks.

Crayola Crayons: Here is another tool that should look pretty familiar to you—the classic crayon! What I love about crayons is the ability to add texture to your lettering. Look at that rough and bumpy texture!

Yoobi Double Ended Colored Pencils: Just like crayons, colored pencils allow you to get a really great texture and give you the ability to add shade to your drawings. They're perfect for coloring books and pages!

LET'S WARM UP

Like any hobby or sport, it is important to warm ourselves up and get our creative juices flowing! Use the space provided to practice some basic shapes. You might even recognize some of them as parts of different letters. Warming up your hand with these simple strokes will get you ready and prepped for the letter drills ahead! Who's ready? Luna is!

let me just finish this cookie first...

When first learning to letter, it's best to start with warm-up exercises to get used to your lettering tool! We do this by drawing simple shapes with your tool of choice to perfect your muscle memory and pressure before drawing actual letters. You'll notice a lot of these warm-up shapes can be put together to create letters! Once you master the shapes, letters shouldn't be scary! Go through the warm-up on the next few pages to get these shapes down!

Lettering is all about learning the muscle movements required to produce each letter and keeping control of your pen. Trust me, my day-to-day handwriting looks nothing like my hand lettering. You do not have to have nice handwriting to be a good letterer!

I don't really believe there is a right or wrong way to hold your tool. I think whatever is most comfortable for you is best. You just want to make sure you aren't gripping too tight and, in turn, making it uncomfortable on any of your fingers. Just find the right position and start moving the tool slowly.

On the next few warm-up pages, you can use the space below each shape to practice drawing your own warm-up shapes.

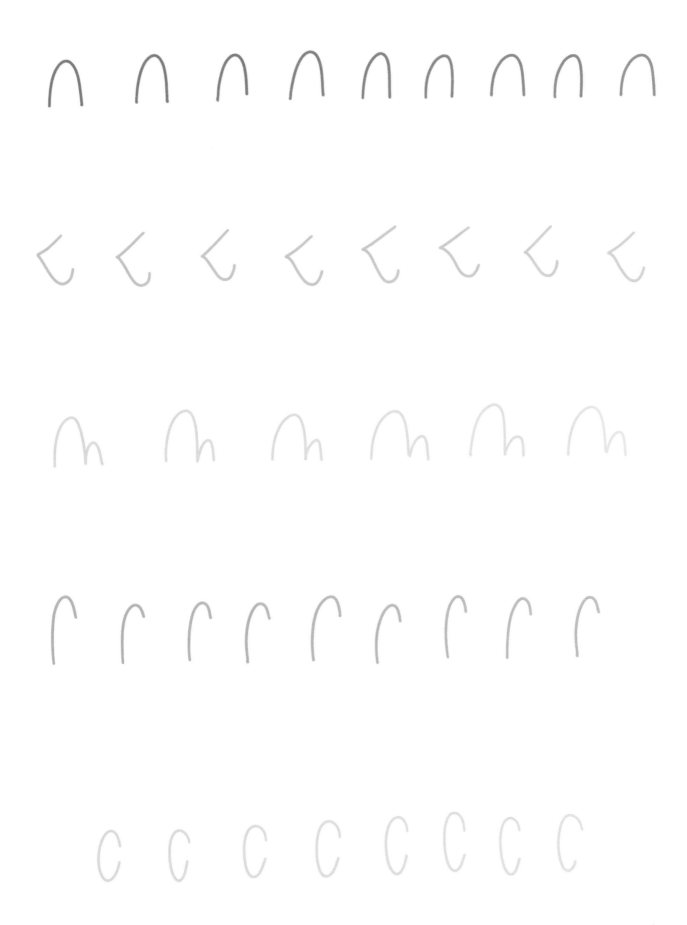

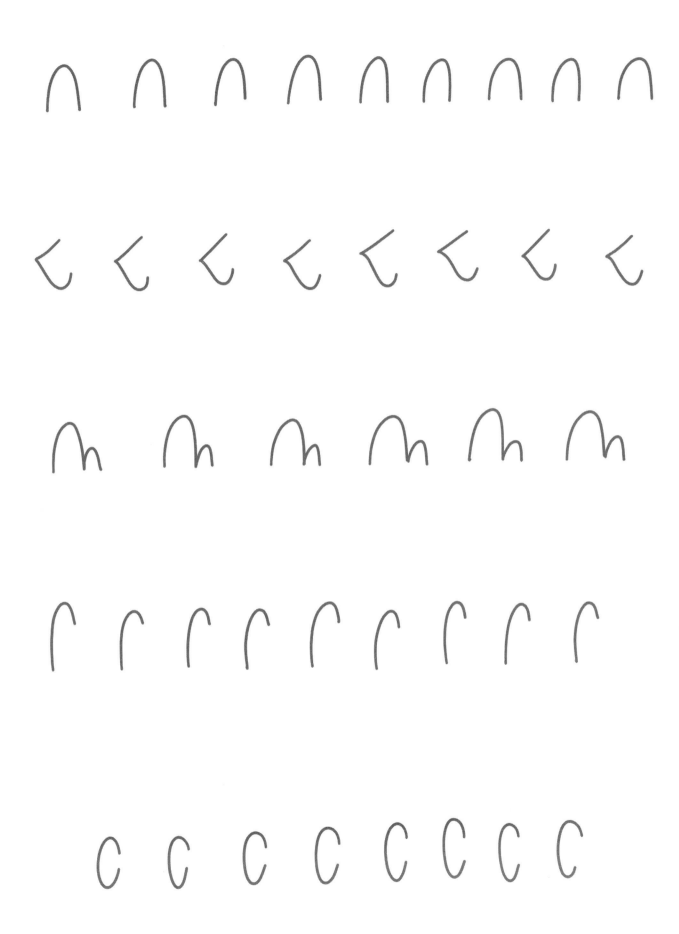

I bet a lot of those shapes felt very familiar to you! And you can probably see where we are going next! Which of the shapes might be put together to create a letter?

Luna's Answer

What do you think? What are some more warm-up shapes that go together to create letterforms? Draw them below!

HOW TO LETTER

In this book, you and Luna will learn multiple styles of lettering.
We will go over six different alphabets, and I will show you how to
change little things about each one to make them different!
On the next page, you'll see how I take a script alphabet and
create "faux calligraphy" by creating thick downstrokes.
(Remember downstrokes from our letter basics?) I will also show you
how to create thicker downstrokes on a plain sans serif alphabet.

One of my favorite alphabets to use in lettering is script. When I draw my script alphabet, my preferred method is working with consistent pressure using a monoline pen. An easy way to change up the look of the script alphabet is adding thick downstrokes. With my style of script lettering, I achieve the traditional calligraphy look by creating my downstroke after I letter my word. This technique can also be used with your sans serif or serif alphabets. This instantly gives you a way to create two different-looking alphabets!

I draw out my letter with pen, pencil, or chalk, and then go back to create thicker downstrokes by drawing a second connecting line on each letter and filling it in. When using thicker tools like chalk and paint pens, this effect can be produced by outlining the downward strokes.

First, I letter the word in script.

Then I follow the curves of each letter and add in my downstrokes.

Above is an example of the incorrect way to create downstrokes with script; instead of following the curve of each letter, I went straight down each time.

LETTER DRILLS

Now that we have warmed up our hands, are you ready to start lettering? You've reached the part of the book that is probably the most exciting! Letter drills! Grab your favorite lettering tool and get ready to start tracing these letterforms. You'll move through multiple alphabets. Start by studying the shape of the first letter, trace the next two, and then try them by yourself in the space provided! Don't worry if your letters don't look just like mine at first. Remember, practice makes progress.

a b c d e
f g h i j
k l m n o
p q r s t
u v w x
y z

a a a

b b b

c c c

d d d

e e e

f f f

30

g g g

h h h

i i i

d d d

k k k

l l l

m m m

n n n

o o o

p p p

q q q

l l l

32

y y, y,

z z z z

How did your first set of letter drills go? Don't worry if they were harder than you thought! It's important to repeat those shapes over and over to commit them to muscle memory. This next section will give you more room to practice. Don't give up!

YOU DID IT!

You and Luna just finished your first alphabet and set of letter drills! Congrats! That is something to celebrate.

Whether you feel happy, discouraged, or frustrated, I want you to know I am proud of you, especially if you keep working through the book! Lettering isn't easy, and it's important to always remember that learning anything new is challenging at first.

Luna is feeling a little discouraged because her letters don't always look exactly like the example, but she is ready to keep moving through the drills and practicing.

This next alphabet should look very familiar. It is the same as the one you just completed, but this time we'll add the downstrokes. Remember, the downstroke creates the look of calligraphy, and this style can be referred to as faux (or fake) calligraphy! Don't forget that the downstroke should follow the curve of your letter. Draw each letterform like you just did in the previous alphabet, and then go back to add in your downstroke.

Good luck. You've got this!

a b c d e
f g h i j
k l m n o
p q r s t
u v w x
y z

42

g g g

h h h

i i i

j j j

k k k

l l l

y *y* *y*

z *z* *z*

m

n

o

p

q

r

y

z

CONNECTING SCRIPT

Woo! Isn't the script alphabet so pretty and fun? It is definitely Luna's favorite. But now that we've practiced those letterforms, we need to learn how to connect them all together to create words!

If you are familiar with cursive, this will look very different to you! When writing in cursive, you write fluidly and keep your pen to your page throughout. When lettering, we look at each letterform as its own shape that needs to be connected to the next letter. We do that a few different ways. The most common is by creating long tails on the end of some of our letterforms. Sometimes there are letter connections where we will keep the pen to paper and stay fluid, like a double "l" or double "e."

Let's go through some of these connections so you can get a better idea of what I mean!

luna

Let's break down Luna's name. Each letter is written separately and connected with the tail of the letter before. You can see where I would connect the letters with the emphasis lines.

Now you try writing "luna" with the extended tails to connect the letters.

luna

Here's another example. With "kate" you break the "t" into two pieces. You get the first part of the "t" with the extended tail of the "a." Once you connect your letters, finish the word by crossing your "t."

Now you try "kate:"

Here's a tricky one! As you can see, the "r's" and the "t" are broken up into two pieces. The first "r" is started by the tail of the "a," and the "r" is then sloped down with the tail extended to create the beginning of the "t." Then the "e" creates the first part of the "r" by the extension of its tail!

Try this tricky one, and then turn the page to try a few more names!

frank

pete

george

wanda

ollie

Ollie might have given you a struggle! That is a lot of loops. That is why we practiced those during our warm-ups. Try that one again!

ollie

It's your turn! Practice connecting the letters of your name.

MORE LETTER DRILLS

A B C D E F G

H I J K L M

N O P Q R

S T U V W

X Y Z

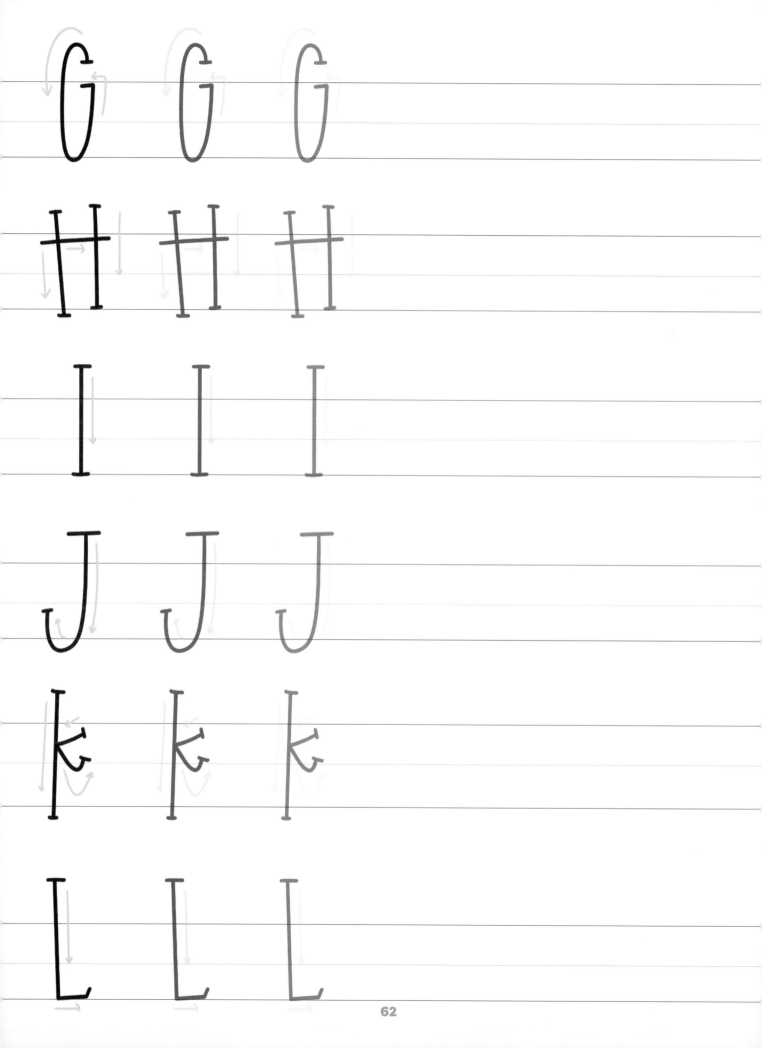

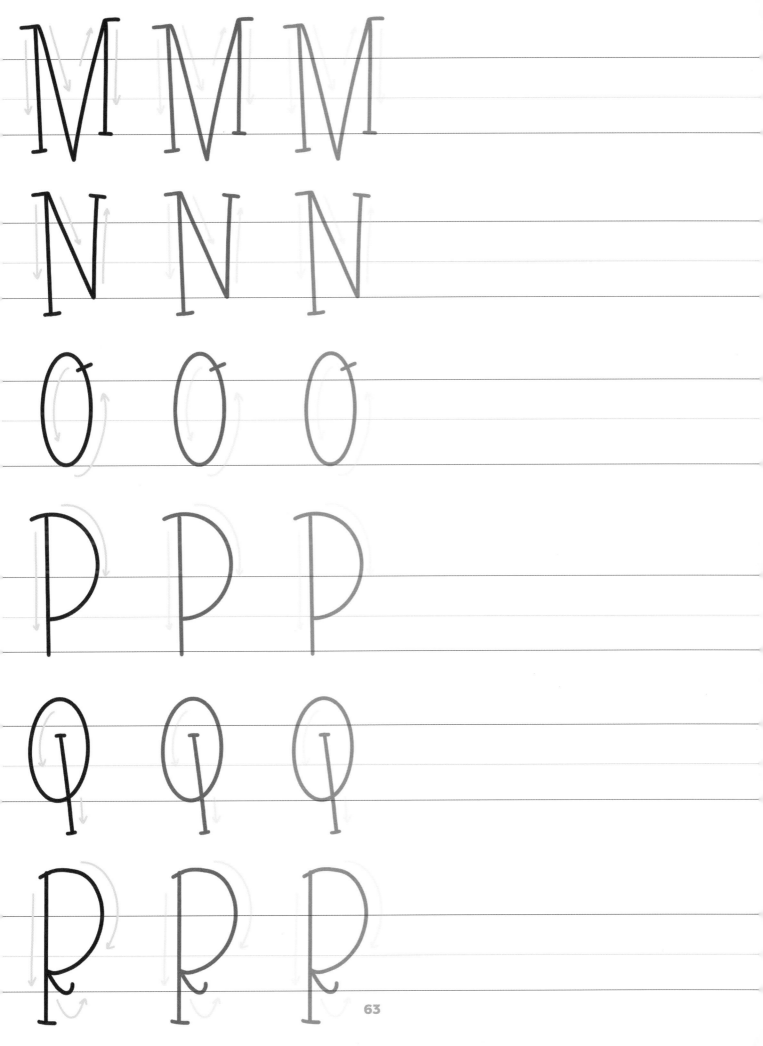

63

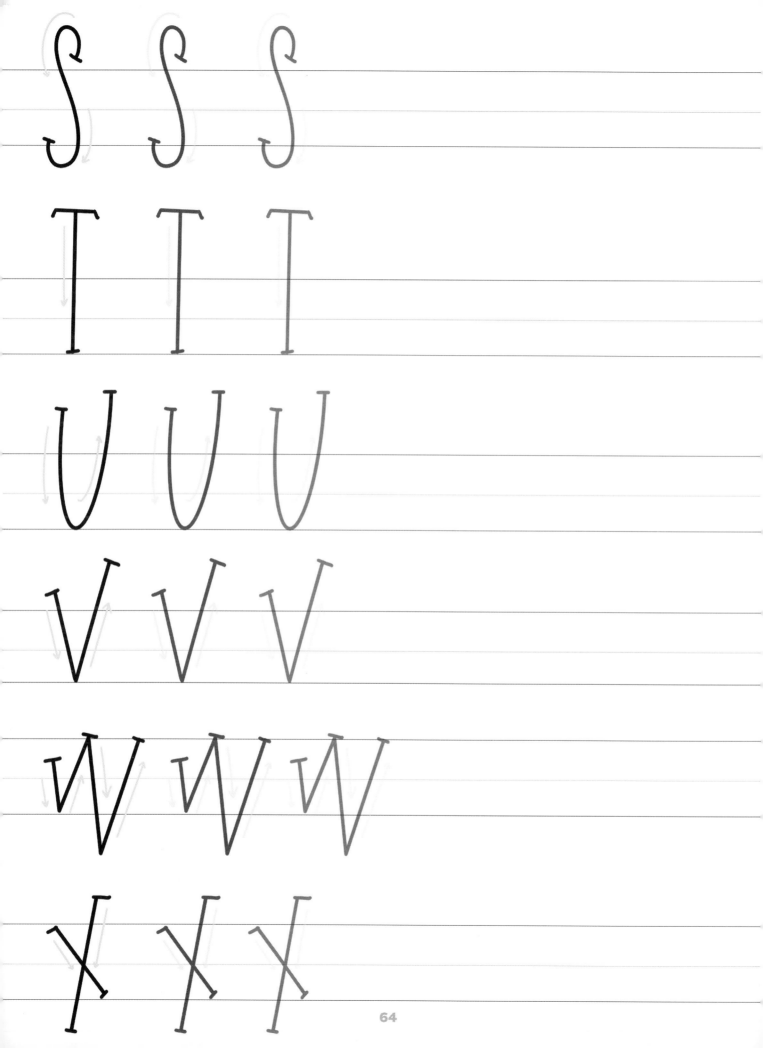

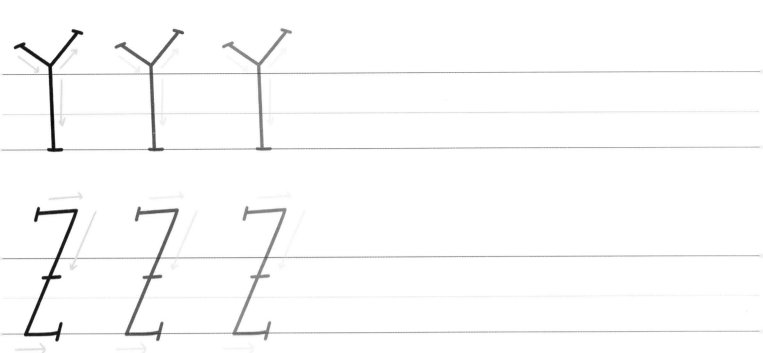

a b c d e f

g h i j k l m

n o p q r s

t u v w x y z

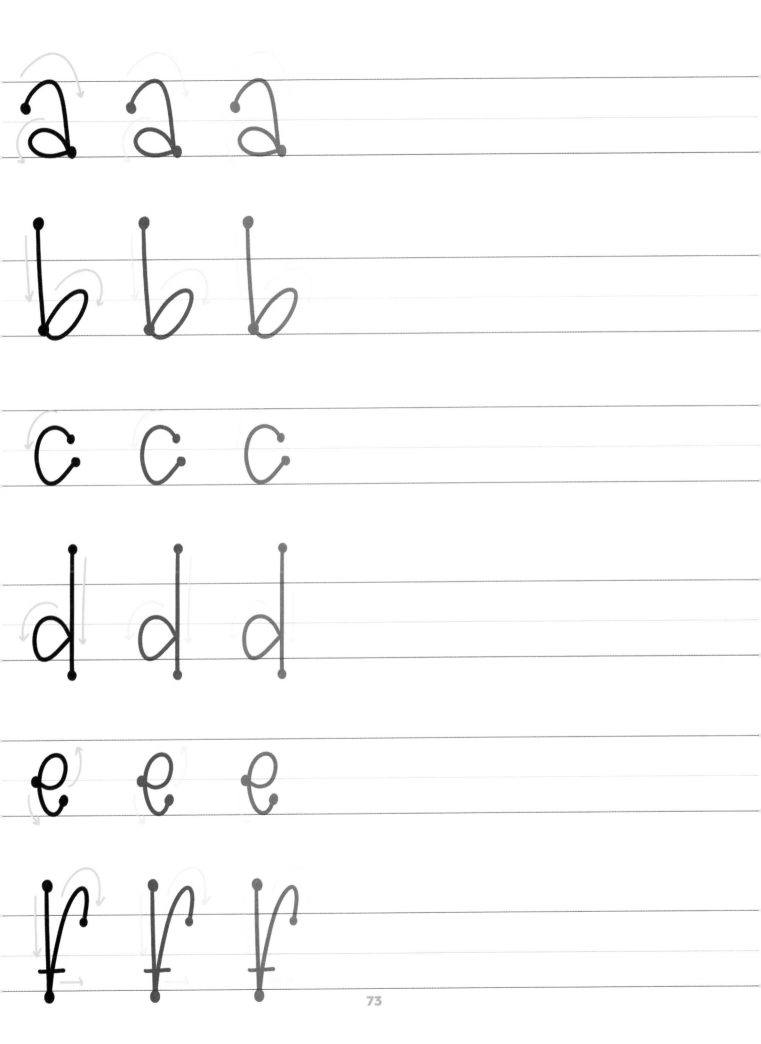

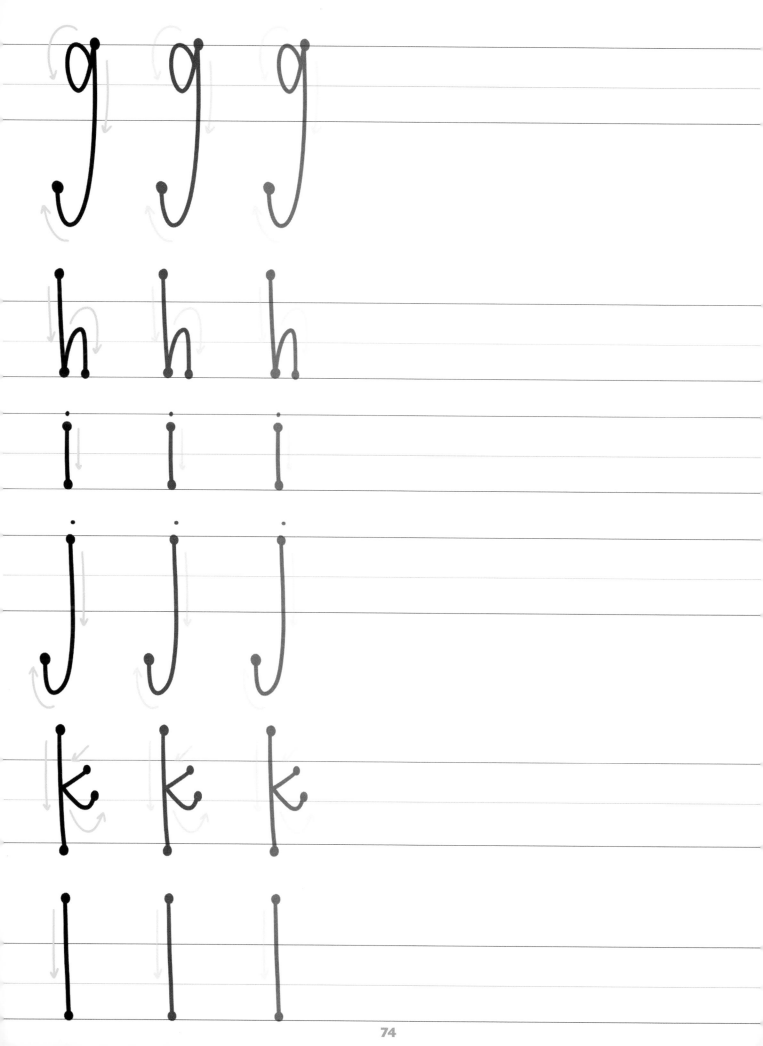

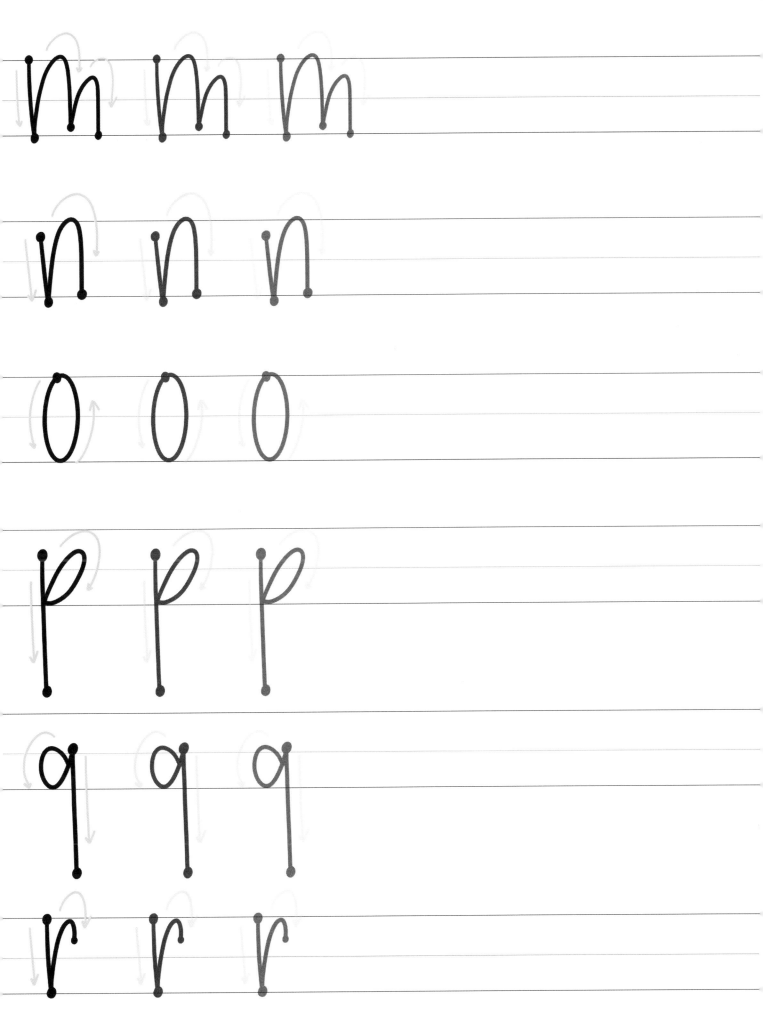

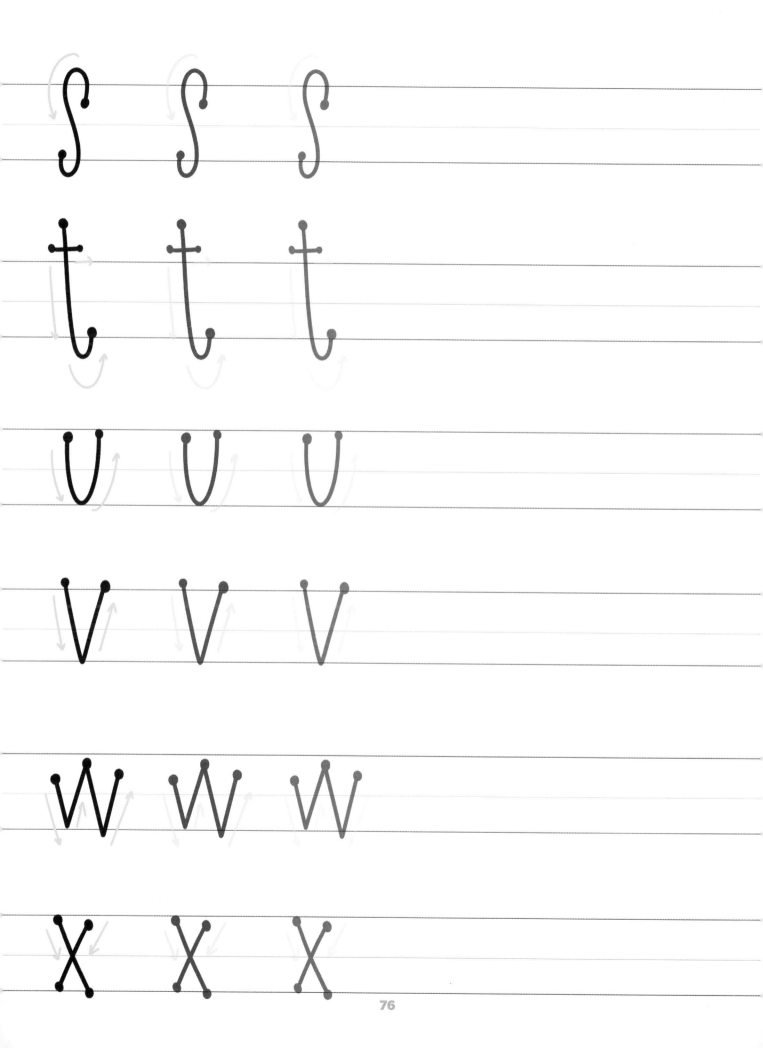

76

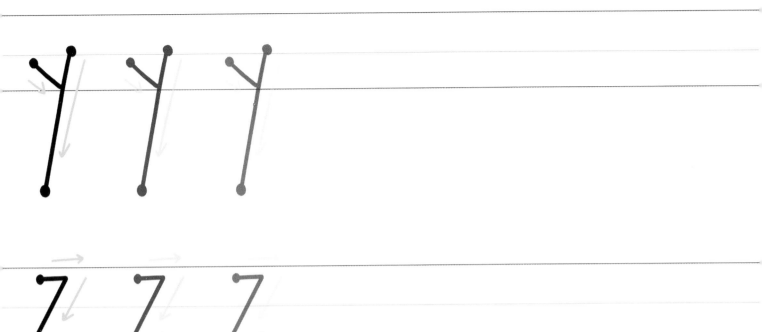

Y

Z

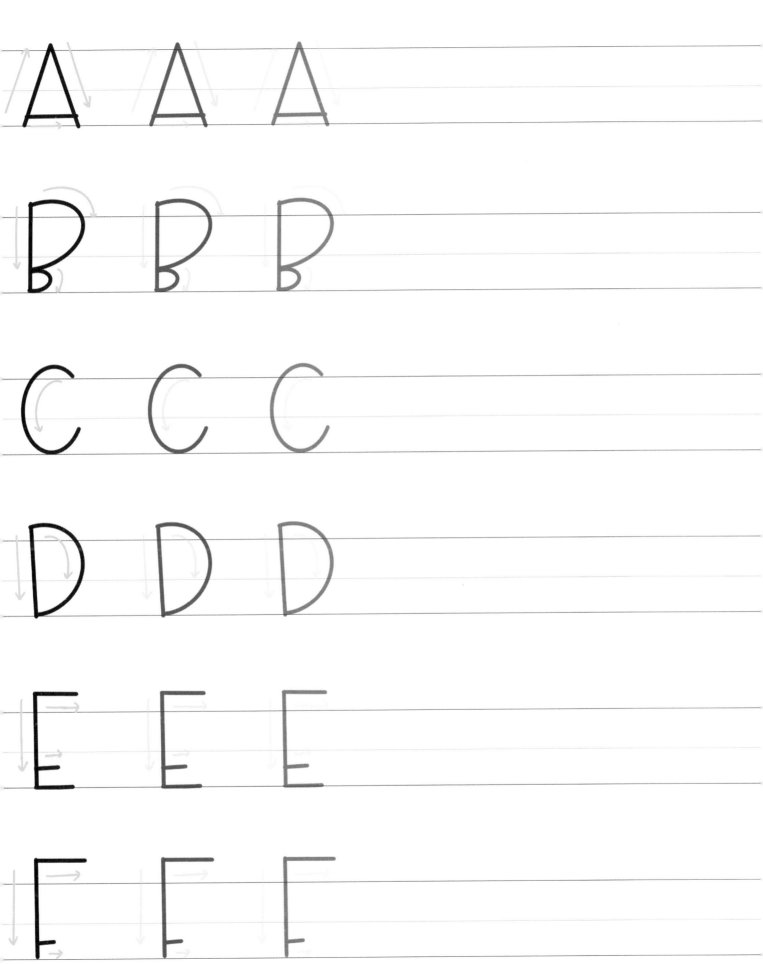

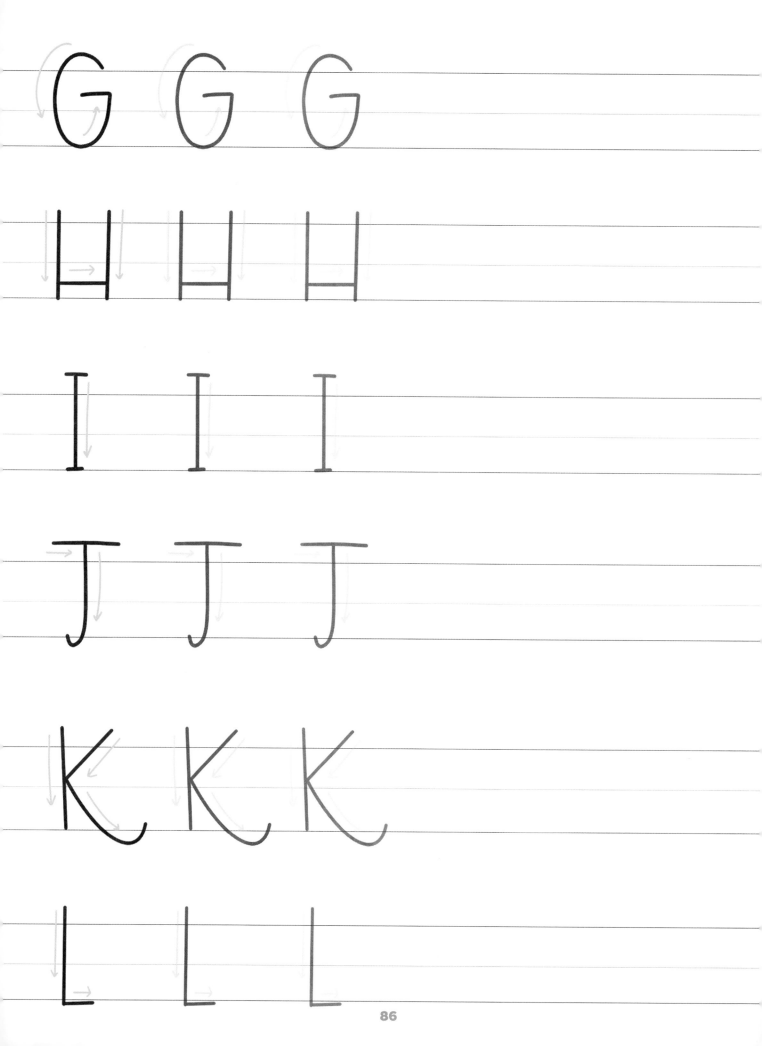

M M M M

N N N N

O O O

P P P

Q Q Q

R R R

Y Y Y

Z Z Z

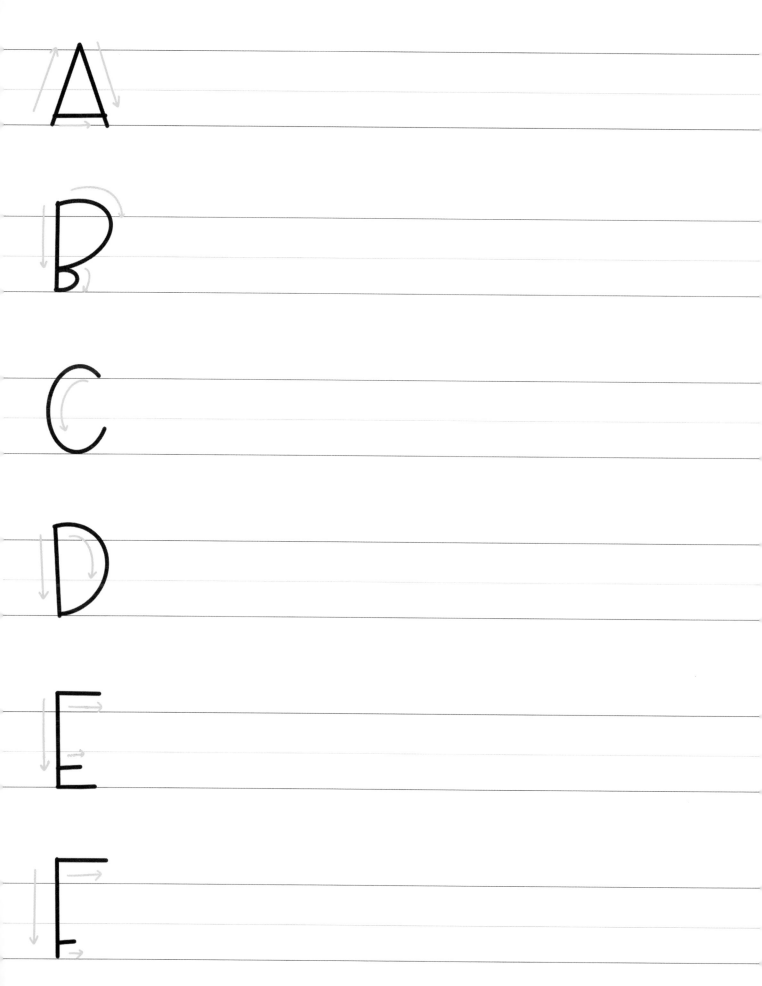

G

H

I

J

K

L

A B C D E F G

H I J K L M

N O P Q R S

T U V W X

Y Z

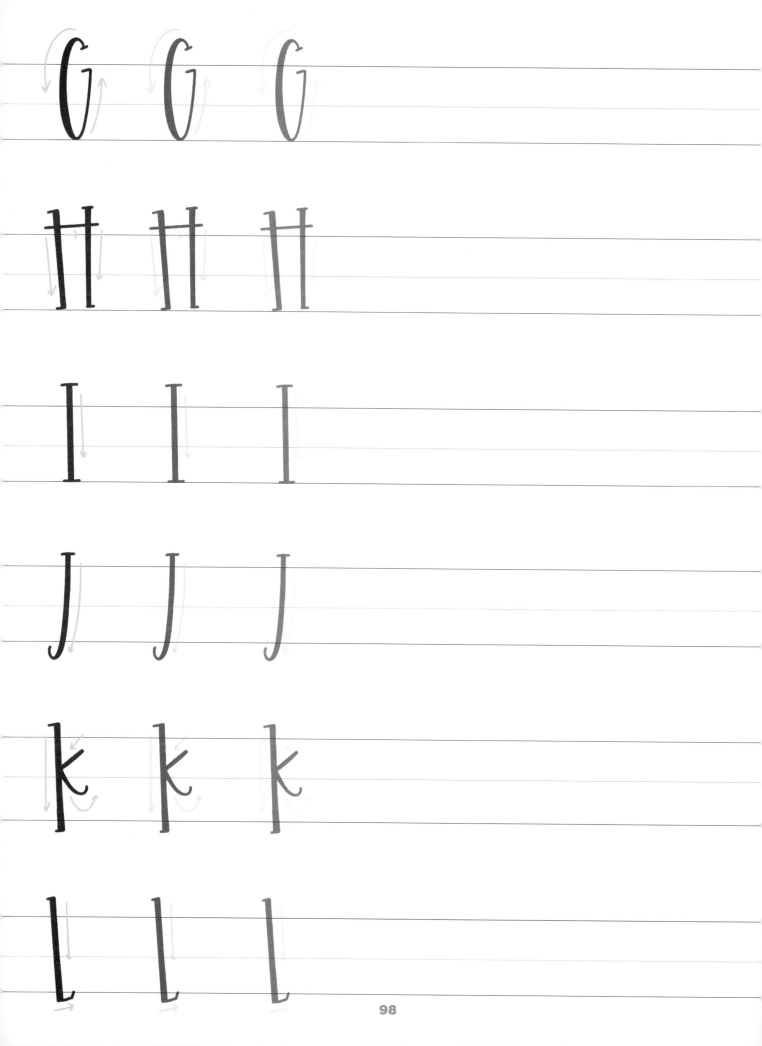

M M M

N N N

O O O

P P P

Q Q Q

R R R

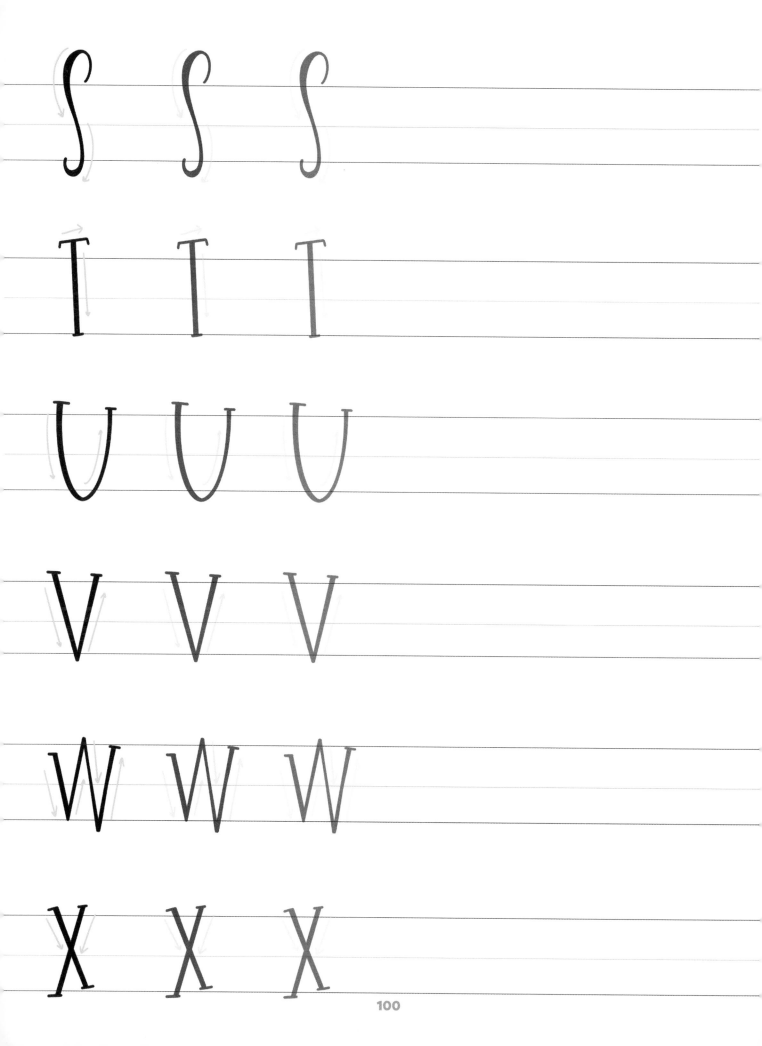

Y Y Y

Z Z Z

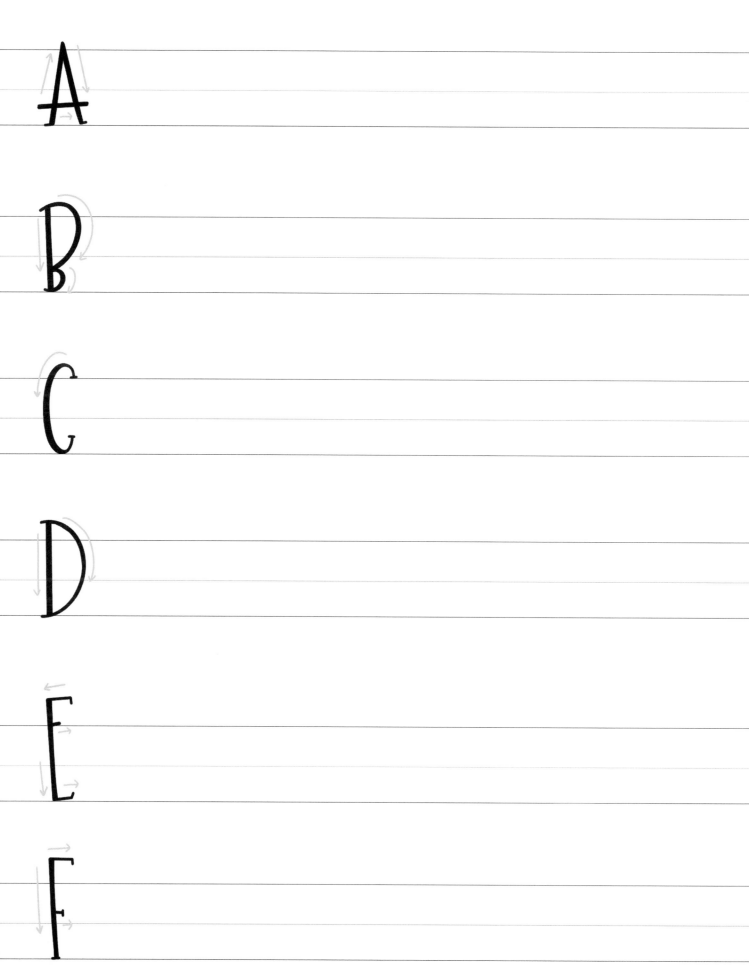

Y

Z

DANCE PARTY

You're invited to the lettering dance party! This section goes over what I like to call making your letters "dance!" This style can also be referred to as "bouncy." So, how do you achieve this dance-party bouncy look?

Here are some of my go-to techniques:
1. Ignore the baseline.
2. Dip your tails.
3. Throw in some loops.
4. Make some letters smaller than others.
5. Exaggerate your descenders and ascenders.
6. Try to be as fluid as possible.

That sounds easy, right? Probably not! These techniques are definitely advanced and will take some time to master. On the next few pages we'll break this style down to help you and Luna understand it better!

When dancing with my script alphabet, I usually ignore the baseline and let at least two of the letters sit on it. For this example, my "p" and "y" are sitting pretty even on the baseline. I dipped my "a" tail and my "t" tail down below the baseline. And I finished the cross stroke with a little flourish! (We will get to that in the following section.)

PARTY

When dancing with my sans serif or serif alphabets, I treat it similarly to the script alphabet and ignore the baseline. I also slant my letters slightly so they aren't straight up and down. In this example, the legs of my "A" are two different sizes!

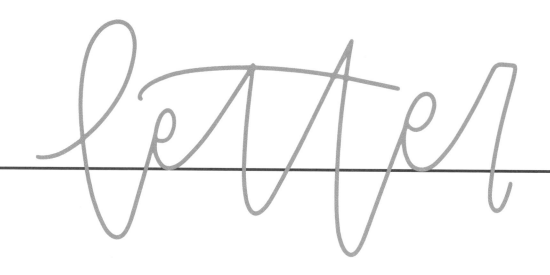

Can you tell me the ways I made the letters dance here?

Luna's Answer

For the first example, you dipped the descender letters below the baseline.

For the second example, you slanted some of the letters and they all sit on differing baselines.

Your turn!

Trace the examples below to practice dancing with your letters! Then try on your own.

silly

SILLY

happy

HAPPY

cheers

CHEERS

birthday

BIRTHDAY

Now you pick! What words do you want to make dance? Try those out here.

MIXING STYLES

We just learned six different styles of lettering and how to make those letters dance! How are you feeling now? Luna is a bit overwhelmed but excited to get to work. Now, how do we get these styles to mix and work together? I am glad you asked!

Mixing and matching different types of lettering can really add to your final design. My favorite kind of alphabet to mix with my script letters is a thin sans serif. Just like the one you learned earlier! An easy rule of thumb to mixing alphabets is to use ones that look opposite. When you do that, the two usually complement each other. If you have a thinner, flowy style, a thicker serif font would match nicely. That being said, there really isn't a right or wrong way to approach it! Just try to get a feel for which two alphabets might look good together!

When you mix alphabets, it helps you say something with your design. Try to evoke a feeling and go with it. To me, serif is a serious typeface. It is level, easy to read, and uniform. Because I find tall, skinny sans serif designs a little sillier, I tend to draw a sans serif to go with playful designs. Let's work through a few different examples of mixing and matching! We'll do a lot of mixing and matching alphabets in the activities at the end of the book with all of Luna's friends!

So let's practice–use the examples to trace and practice on your own!

girl
POWER

girl
POWER

HAPPY
birthday

HAPPY
birthday

SPREAD
love

SPREAD
love

You are doing great! Use this space to keep practicing what you've learned or to try mixing new words and styles.

FLOURISHES + DOODLES

If you want to step up your lettering designs, add in some fun flourishes or illustrations! They can be used to emphasize what you are trying to say or fill in blank space in your design. I love using natural elements like plants or wreaths as illustrations. Another great lettering enhancer is a banner. Just like your letterforms, these simple illustrations are made up of pretty simple shapes. They may take some time to get used to, so use the space provided to trace and practice!

You may have noticed that some of my letters don't look exactly like the ones you practiced in your letter drills! That's because sometimes, I add a little flourish or design to a letter to give it a different look and feel.

This section of the book has Luna pretty nervous, because flourishes can be pretty tricky! Don't be discouraged if it does not come natural to you. It doesn't come naturally to Luna either. You really need to devote time and energy to perfecting this skill! Flourishes are definitely not necessary to being a great letterer. They can, however, dress up a word or letter in a fun and whimsical way!

With flourishes, less is more. They are usually used on the first and last letter of a word. They can also be added to descender letters or letters that require cross strokes (check back to our vocab lesson in your letter basics section!). Just like little illustrations, flourishes can be used to fill open space in your overall design. Make sure they enhance your design and don't overcomplicate it! Remember, certain letterforms begin or end similarly, so once you master a flourish for one letter, you can apply it to others.

Let's start by practicing some simple doodles and banners! Use the next few pages to trace and practice!

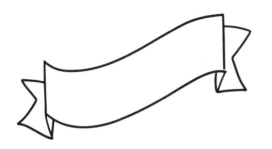

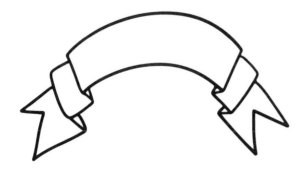
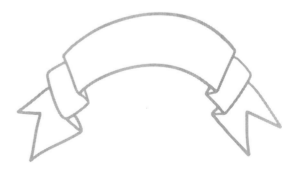

Now, let's work on some flourishing! Remember, keep your flourishes simple. This will help keep your words easy to read. Use the space provided to practice some of my favorite flourished letters. Take your time and trace the examples, then practice on your own!

This is the type of "j" I might start a word with. I angle it a little more and create a swoosh downstroke that would go under my second letter.

This "k" is another example of how I would start a word, or even use in the middle of the word and not connect it to the next letter.

Here's a great example of how I would end a word with the letter "o," like "hello." I just add a little flourish to the end!

Practice Page

Practice Page

ACTIVITIES

It's time to meet all of Luna's friends! Let's put everything we learned into practice with some fun activities! You'll see a completed design, a traceable design, and one for you to fill in however you would like! Get creative and try out your new skills!

zack the zebra zig zags thru the field

zack the zebra zigzags thru the field

Kate the KOALA kicks back under the PALM tree

Kate the
Koala
kicks back
under the
»PALM«
tree

SUSAN THE SLOTH sings silly songs

SUSAN THE SLOTH sings silly songs

OLLIE THE OCTOPUS ONLY drinks STRAWBERRY smoothies

OLLIE
THE
OCTOPUS
ONLY DRINKS
STRAWBERRY
SMOOTHIES

PETE the penguin EATS A LOT OF pickles

PICKLES

PETE the penguin EATS A LOT OF pickles

PICKLES

TOLEYLA LOVE
KHLOE. ♡ ♡

146

HAL {THE} HEDGEHOG HAS TWO LEFT FEET

HAL [THE] HEDGEHOG
HAS TWO LEFT FEET

maies

george the giraffe bakes german chocolate cake

george the giraffe bakes german chocolate cake

mom LOVE

FRANNY

the flamingo

FLOATS
IN

floats

THE

pool

FRANNY
the flamingo
FLOATS
IN
THE
pool

frank the fox fancies fried chicken

frank the fox
fancies fried
chicken

Thank you so much for hanging with Luna and me throughout this whole book! We hope you had such a great time learning a new skill. Now it's time to get creating. Remember all the things you can do with your new lettering? Make someone a special card, decorate your notebooks, add some razzle-dazzle to your next school project, or create a fun craft for yourself. The possibilities are endless!

ABOUT THE ILLUSTRATOR

I'm Kelsey Davis: freelance illustrator living mostly in Oklahoma City, sometimes in Seattle, once in Costa Rica for a bit. Favorite things include savory breakfast foods, laying in the sun, sloths, exploring new places with my husband, Danny, and making a really good cup of coffee. Kelsey Davis @kelseydavisdesign